# THE LEGACY OF
# THOMAS LEPERA

THOMAS LEPERA

# THE LEGACY OF THOMAS LEPERA

STONEWALL PRESS
PAVING YOUR WAY TO SUCCESS

Published in the United States of America

ISBN: 978-1-949362-68-8 (*sc*)
978-1-949362-67-1 (*e*)

Library of Congress Control Number: 2018955108

Stonewall Press books may be ordered through booksellers or by contacting:

Stonewall Press
4800 Hampden Lane, Suite 200
Bethesda, MD 20814 USA
www.stonewallpress.com
1-888-334-0980
orders@stonewallpress.com

Short Stories
19.03.15

# CONTENTS

I, Adonis ........................................................................ 9

In Greek mythology Adonis is a figure of mystery. He is an annually-renewed, ever-youthful god bearing a life-death-rebirth deity. He is the archetype to handsome youth.

Her Soigné ........................................................................19

We do hope you enjoy the oldest uncertainty renown to test mankind's prudence starting, let's say, circa 3,000 BC and notably ongoing nonstop today, i.e., prospects of vow and ring binder, whichever limits, can define a certain ending to the former self and riot curiously sacrosanct toward new life beginning.

Cesarean's Bad Mistress ............................................49

This's a physiological twister from being disgruntled when to learn his fishwife has better dreams but for him culminating in outright rejection from the ante room.

Witches of Endau....................................................57

We must fight off those cruel witches who inhabit the neighboring cemetery. They rakishly rejoice in taking body parts for their own outlandish amusement.

Wily Rabbit..........................................................63

Chronicles of Wily Rabbit deliver an anecdote by saying the best years of our lives is probably between ages 4 years old and 12. Psychologists tend to agree that these revealing years are more significant than we can imagine. Personalities develop at an alarming rate but physiology suggests an absurd body change beginning with puberty leaves behind the best years.

# FOREWORD TO ADONIS

In Greek mythology Adonis is a figure of mystery. He is an annually-renewed, ever-youthful god bearing a life-death-rebirth deity. He is the archetype to handsome youth.

After 4,500 years of dead silence it is time to usher in his voice.

# I, ADONIS

BY THOMAS LEPERA

Though time seems so adverse and means unfit, though wayward fortune did malign the fair harbor in my house, these thoughts most sincere they wound my worse than sword my flesh. Traitors flock to tempest themselves with howling winds to bring out all discomfort. A great contention of sea and sky is in this broiling hamlet. Yet in these thoughts throughout despair and menace I doth modest marvel how to steal away my frightful thoughts. 'Tis neither a gift nor praise fitted to have spoken thereof this thought is a loss which cannot choose itself. As her eyes did gaze, insinuate not, there is but guiltless import above suspicion amongst these gaunt days. To chide my haunt my troubled reply had I myself chose to absolve the adored life of this poor player we find a faultless end. Let ruling senses cleave to that my fed bounty taste, I guess the sequel. Strange solace but queer in fortune's womb that has watered this suffered sorrow. He knew not well but guessed it was she.

Its scorns' reproach to lie most hidden but for who's meaning the greater: their distain of a sparrow's flight or perhaps I to reason fully my deep murk? I do beguile the thing I am by seeming otherwise. Has it not been misfortune's stillness to trial then come with spun out heart's deep languor? No wounded vanity was ever contented by grief but ill will is maddened in pique. In few whose spirit is but fire if any think brave outweighs bad choice, wistfulness lays mirror on her likeness an untimely frost. Alas, to suffer under this vengeful bane, why now the tragedy wots so tirelessly in fame whilst others thou basely slain in brawls. Cruel tears canker and see when as comes to witness that sorrow craves pardon at my hand. By what though has gone before how well the sequel hangs together, I suffer the pangs. Unto these sorrows, why then as I guess, I do escape to such love not sorrow but another.

How well its nightmare did fasten fay my thoughts. Their pounding glee when they together carnivals make uplifts a galling ache. What though bragging and telling of fantastical lies she canst not affect such for idly prating as what delight is there to stare upon dooming perdition? To see heaven's forbid, I know the devil's trumpet sound to succeed in such destiny. We may guess by this one day she should fly away leave all madness to yesterday. Why live life from unease to dread? What reason when offing comes dismissed with tersest "no"? Unseal such senses to good verdict to see the stifling cause of lunacy is to deny it. Now I douse out suchlike strife to end this recreant affair. For come this in hamlet these trifling dames quite mad see only thin gruel. I guess one angel in another hell. Sheathe thy sword, here and now, I'll pardon evermore thee myself to seek without mortal woe to expiate and then abridge much mournful days. Tis destiny untenable and sits at my heart for in my sleep what dreams may come on us than canst not enter but by love.

What I did lament had contempt unto a flanking exploit whose bestowed life of what ill untamed beating heart did temper hard the strongest in our censure. A fisherman of Corinthian deity did scorn, what is most dear who's footing here espying as nit of others, "be quiet for every goose is cackling". Believe me for that was my meaning what vile temperance would be of this dire sport. Many stands in number though in reckoning none and on it bestowed more contrite tears. What though hast called her to a reckoning in sadness I am sorry for my sake you have suffered all this. I am ill of reckoning for this I owe you, but the comfort is in the end of reckoning. Come to me at your convenient speed take conclusion with embassy of meeting me. I choose the eddy taking to fend my melan-maelstrom; this burning call heard well to doff their low pomposity and shake off the slumber of my repose. Within sea storm midst canst we not rally yet again tomorrow's glow to take once more? How mutiny is rankled in my bold senses. If ghoulish scorn may mull this retreat adrift on a sea uncharted, I offer most laudable swear, to stand against thy sight, surely, I to be loved by thee was made tender by thy stunning comeliness. And the tremor of any life's creation reveals itself in lovely form. It is fairer than our eyes can see. To borrow cupid's wings, let what appears most comely mistress then my eyes doth feast to entertain times with thoughts of brawling dreams of love.

Should *I, Adonis*, with inflaming sole effect to live again and breathe such myths vow as to swear more temperate by my lips by what fate that love in heaven's bliss was willing to tend and stay beyond. The open era of youth doth listen softly to thy rising senses, how whisperings riot an unvetted fervor. Ah, I allay at the sight o' the child, his silence of unsullied innocence persuades me when speaking fails. To this hour no guess in knowledge no one so unwise did share it. Was not lascivious manner taken in dread and we knew not of ill-doing nor dreamt the burden in these unfledged days have made. I canst not cast a trammel on such lingering doom made certain to waste thyself upon their vice. We'll answer who first sinned with us thou never spoke to better purpose.

It's a time to try man's soles. Time for all things which perforce without lapsing whose worst was folklore and widely spoke tales. Whatever thyself mirrors own pleasing that's not feigned she is but naïve in comportment but not guilt-ridden of else more. Perceive not her hamlet curse she is a fervent girl, a lovely ingénue to stand title among us. None like these slatterns have gone before us, do not infer, as I have not impugned blame. I therefore do not vow inevitable fault against their shame, nor never shall mistress be of it. Ragged spite dares to bring thievish progress of fools you are deceived. Mayst my thoughts draw closer akin to her likeness? The hour runs through the moral day the morning wears on be dashed with gloomy rain. Some relish for the saltness of today now debated with decay we've lost our wary joy. Shepherds envious of the lamb to step soon with the noiseless foot of time the lady has no folly she'll keep no hoodwink till she is married. My senses make their repair to open the eyes of lifespan choice else sorrow is vetted toward ourselves. To whom I am so infinitely bound in my gentle senses else better pleased with madness. Did I invocate that affable familiar pale ghost my confessor in memory he holds a prevalent seat? At whose approach but few now living can behold mortal ghost to haunt me still, let him pass.

As dawning day in bated breath obedient right of cordial cheer reaps my thanks. Obscured course awaking every man be master in time of action will find fit rewards our secret be undone be well assured. Why such impress of shipwright whose wrongly miscreate sore task then whose right is worthiest purchase your instincts. Spent all my time waiting in silent reveries I'll find restful hush bound in thoughts of living. With thy own birthright, trusting few my innocence fails me, too well conceited, let us go. Let me be thought in my fret shall I rue my heart? However, I am to think of obedient lot that fear still sentinels over right, um, I think not. More than I, my will to never pilfer any fearsome thoughts, fear nothing. Wherein you see me fear not me.

More than I dread loss, dismay is most accursed unseal these tidings stand by me. Should doubt to seize me, trust not myself, for fret does betray. Let me be with thought to hate that in fear's outrage I hold no counsel with it. We shall see none to fear's deepest winter. To find loves' sweet promise fly away from here in the arms of winged angels they'll take me there. My living upon her faith usurps thy casting thence come what may noble spirit. Untwist the strands forbear the unlaid pale ghost. Never have I seen a timelier parted ghost patiently absurd. Let a glazed tongue lick the candied folly buff their most absurd intent. Alas, my pale ghost my confessor does despair. Poor thing waxed as pale ashes for woe alas so pale wan eyes. Where lovers are to whisper the virtue of my will, to you I am bound to yours to save my life. Fear did but trifle. Wherever stout boughs bend with fruit as it must with summer's ripening breath, sighs within my lips, she comes through such condign gates of Rouen may op' where faith was fixed converted from things it once was without the burn of turning aside. With all best parts to compass such boundless love and obey to stand level return me to my leading star unfold the very utmost bound I proffer what charms yield up thy gemmed crown.

**END**

# FOREWORD

Thomas LePera has written a stirringly shrewd and rare play with imparted errands of undertaking nuptials. Claudius urgently feels desire for a new life. Opinions are held post by the church; by construal of bachelors' warnings, and denoted rebuttals by the main character, sirrah Claudius. Wiles by players are oftentimes ironic annotations weighing if marriage is a cerecloth wrapped prophecy with deep rooted identity conjectures of unseen naiveté. We do hope you enjoy the oldest uncertainty renown to test mankind's prudence starting, let's say, circa 3,000bc and notably ongoing nonstop today, i.e., prospects of vow and ring binder, whichever limits, can define a certain ending to the former self and riot curiously sacrosanct toward new life beginning.

In LePera's playwright staging of *Her Soigné* the wording effort is stepped up markedly in the stylized script of 17th century with inimitably concise dialogue among three main characters. In *Her Soigné'* he deftly drafts a single-act play from first to last in his spirited prose typically not found in a lot of vignettes. Safeguarding *The English Language Arts* to the author is an ardent curiosity. The idiom text is quite slanted toward diverse style and rousing discourse among brothers.

# HER SOIGNÉ

BY THOMAS LEPERA

***Hector***

***"Come Thee See Here"***

Our travels seek the pelagic yacht Xebec. Morn's dawn tells of footfall sea swells and casting spewer. A summer Foehn gusts these pebbled sullen shores and sandy lay. What soldier's graves are these, their shadows seem sickly pallid preys. What raison d'être, waifs and strays, was in use so far away? That I gainsay the deed, how may be a wound to heal, nay this trouble is not forgotten. But bequeathal honor, 'tis not so, as if not as you have stomach to find a solace cheer. The solemn sorrow infers not this untitled battlement as upwelling tussocks mire its hallowed cause. Heaven's strife is bound in sloughy shallows. As chilling vista of this sight, these tidings another day shan't comfort well. We bade a tryst and tearful farewell.

*Talus…*

> ***"Perfect days in awe delight are filled with candid fantasies."***

How vernal solstice and belated days had spawned my tout and tattle we dare not try to say. Of legacy leitmotif time diaries when seaboards' twilight told a waggish roué beneath shades of willow branches. Gauche times what ornery sonnet is a fever wailing still. Oceans' salty spindrift connives my longing for lank narrative in song, more laughter and meadowlarks in the gloaming.

*Hector…*

> ***"Its peaty sedges ageless as the sun raising each fine morning."***

Call to mind the spumy surf wept long in hardest roars, our enemy raised the vilest atrocities against us who engaged his ravages of war unto all the cities of Ammon. Head stones strewn amid aged elms recall the decade this very leave when tyrants raised its banners of chaos and set fire to the rain. Days of wild laughter of horses and a thousand swords how many had gone to battle, and no one returns. They pursued métier to serve wily and brutal Lords of War. Huns had sowed on horrid tors the carnage of innocents and the March of Victory. It was here allies under harrows of iron, under plow axes, lost their names. Waters now lave life-shores. Oceans have no waste. Grassy marsh-elders in ashen myrtle ready its registrar. Perdu, intern to soldiers' spoil, is sullen in sightless gawp now glowers unstinting hours to lands-end. To fasten in our thoughts that they had courage, our army lain ready to give up their bootless ghosts. Their doubts are conspirators who never sleep death but argue still upon the mournful doubts prevail vain in doubtful triumphs. In such festering commune the overlooked age shall make wailing woes upon thy life to end doubt by death. They lie in company of hoary graves but cannot say to from whence mother and home. Only the deeming cause and 38$^{th}$ Afoot vestige sadly in print.

***Talus…***

> ***"Who goes yonder, there? Who goes slovenly? Is it Zephyr?'***

Whose image even but now appears to us? Wherever quarrels impugn waters' rightly tribune, she comes haughty sylph-like upon crusted sands. Her soigné, a fresco by Monet, had betided my shy resolve. Of mine own eyes what thou usurp this time of night? Whose withdrawal 'tis mine. Haughty eyes threaten to sow discord among brothers. So, angelica was her naïf beauty as a perfect creature sent down in scorn of nature. I'm muted in awe by modish godsend. But my awe is faint-hearted and lowly forlorn in dread. By heart's deep languor, her augury in all hell's taunt, she sings a faint hush to respite heart. She comes basely forsworn ignoble treachery at Claudius.

***Claudius…***

> ***"Talus, it must be truly her febrile corpse. Zephyr is dead."***

I shut out her tetchy chic. I recall a bête-noire, her stilted come hither. I refuted her truculent dictum; yet under dull recount we drank a fitting recherché staging to raise the tempest of outrageous fortune. For aught we know wayward fortune did malign obedient right.

***Talus…***

> ***"Zephyr didn't die. Monsignor Bruno Gucci was nearest at the Opera. She walks on, each stride piercing morns' light."***

Needlepoint and pennant, sun filled tapestry, are ensigns of her gypsy's pith herewith nostrums as performer gormlessly singing a lullaby. Alas, my cumbered land is perused. Curse the day! Here and now, none others smite us, neither time nor bond, save redounding to saccharine smell of Arras fields. Though swear the witticism be laughable, I merit, we cannot be jaded by surfeit in aster fields. There's no thwart hostile to clatter spurning fettle by trig gait. Weird the matter is gaily songs whilst battering daydreams. Woe the foreboding day!

***Claudius…***

> ***"Look upon her vain swaggers; she saunters it, to then fro. God's angels, devoir to honor, shan't protect us nor keep us."***

No coxswain to steer safeway, she'll deign with urbane sophistry most layperson's tenets. Clerics pray shrift that dismaying blame but blind to the darkness within themselves. I mewl contritely at their muse. Either we or they must lower lie. Note well, then, I will speak lower. Mayn't we expose its canon to light a churlish world? Hoarding imprisoned angels appear to men like light but how my comportments recoil. Angels will howl out human frailty as such as host, they plead grace to defend us. Angels warble to rest. Bending angels, it's absurdity alike to another end. But my boldness shan't defend living on a prayer to the everlasting gods. They are deaf to peevish vows. Master thus with bending sickles else a grim abyss awaits in humbly kissing their feet. Whose vows goodwill do contest swordsmen to flail on shrift's blame 'tis to shatter their muse.

***Hector...***

> ***"Have your angels remove this dearth and moorage image."***

With me as elsewhere this issue diverts sagacious courage. Let's not bemuse this turbid dithering. Making worse what nature made so clear being fond of praise makes your praises worse. Worse poison to men's soul a loathsome world thou art deceived do import trial to enter in thoughts of desperate men's penury. Aren't her facile ways, a sage likeness frothing bash in mirth, sent even now to ring knell the ominous rapt of life? In note, be most cautious to her mettle does subsist whichever treacle or by matey. How earnestly are you set a-work and how ill requited? I am lost in the labyrinth of my spiteful execrations —lost all the serpentine craft of my caduceus-which ignorance itself knows is so foist abundant a curse. Fools are like husbands' fault that lies what duty they do owe, thus mock and take your commission. Polluted with lusty desire it taints chaste wonders whilst you judge it a thing impossible. Will nothing turn your unrelenting infirmity? Would it be otherwise that I could thrash him whilst he railed at me? My live is better ended if that makes calamity. There, wherever my violable sufferings subsist, my mislaid life dies a most doomed affair.

***Talus…***

> ***"Abbey's sacramental shriving has paid no chutzpah split. Satan comes thusly afoot to devour flesh".***

They wear pelf cassocks, of pinned collars, the look of it haute-kitsch in seminary rustly windows. Abbey's shriving, indistinct from its oily perfidies, is to fatuous rank attests. In beard and gown, they are but gluttonous as puffins in full dress. Graven idols had cozened our reveries whist by sloth and ruttiest verse. *By gar* cozened be in service is an unjustly win. To bridge a roadway to providence with virtuous praise as valor's monuments does spur his future with past deeds. Throughout said deeds darkly answered most persisted deeds a hollow welcome does not defend him, all pity choked and ransom ill deeds. Angst the Rise of Lucian sought by canon's aim, hence we repose Amdahl's lance of steel calms our tiredest wait. Pay no levy, no tithe, nor worth to us.

***Hector…***

> ***"No truer words. Zephyr is led by Abbey vow and privilege."***

There is vast abatement of outlook should my lofty duty be faint. Alas, are there not chivalric innocents harmed in scurfy privileges gone wrongly? We wish hence to redact strongly such thrown daring. If togged sibyl may confess, ask wilt exalted titles-conferred by our holy basilica- lay the vanward fete. Fools are doting in envy. What fondly jealousy ripened to impose inheritable envy to shun my fair path. Oh, weary reckoning heavy reckoning I am ill for this I owe but not yet of mind to call Claudius to a reckoning for she is shrewder than he. A fickle fortune smiled on poor discontents 'tis giddy fortune's grace of her he follows. Must there no more be done to rebuff lies howling sweet maid her virgin chants. Zephyr by achy vow yet promised mealy is, say truth, a doubted maenad. If immunity guides vows, if vows are sanctimonies, if there is rule in itself, this was not she. There is madness of discourse that sets of strange natures where reason can revolt and yet assume all reason. This is itself unassailable and it is not.

***Claudius…***

> ***"Be most sentient. Jollity is her scepter after all, is it not?"***

Wouldn't it be hubristic to see false outset made conspicuous in our eyes by wry irony? My self-confidence is but usual in womanly chorus but hostile to Abbey's scurry constrains to doting habits. Even at holy vicarage she is unreservedly detached from utile chapters. She is, in say truth, herself an outlier artisan—neither town nor shire follower. It's her purlieu singularity to take hold of fates' pated heart. Till now my char grousing cannot yet openly vitiate fraud faulty and I prefer to rob my scarce rewards. We are cautious; per contra I see she's unctuous. Oughtn't we to take pique of her plotting intrigue? To the end of reckoning for love to aye endure, yea, we circumspect to cloying smiles that lay a pastiche. My reasoning ends volte-face in yield to chaste feeling and I live fain to my instincts and writhe to these ends. My revel not cozened nor beguiled if the vicar meant rebels fickle is hereon ended.

***Hector...***

> ***"Halt this potent she-devil that puissant comes.***
> ***Hide from view thyself. Use your nom de plume,***
> ***nom de guerre."***

What monger sated to slake our bond trots the air. As craven a shrewd wind given beside common sense what monger is wotted? Do thou profess thyself a knave or a fool and yet subscribe for thee art both knave and fool? What though is he for a fool to bear a shambling maiden trot? This dame to stand forth usurer grew puissant hostile to the strings of life. Bemoaning her blush to whisper me, such comely chorus tolls my discontent. No such matter of another's dotage but does not appetites alter and awe a man? Come I here from a princely station to know your anguishes wherein demands are just. You raise me up to more than I can be. Till I am free buy nothing of me. To do slander and behold his sway in therewithal what cheer, madam? Why should calamity be full of words. Her tongue offends a privilege and more much more time will bring it out. Ruthless debt contemns fulfillment and I shan't pay. I cannot sacrifice my hardened suffrage, the rightly reason, and prefer the verdict of ettle thinking. Socrates pondered well noble leaders ought not to be quickened in spontaneity. Is it not wise to ply the rule? Buy reason and sell off makeshift hours made serendipitous, dear brother. That wants discourse you are no truant. Come away! Stand where the torch light cannot discern us. Incontinent rogue comes nattily when love 'tis due then begs a kiss. By a dainty beckoning, she comes to appear at you.

***Claudius…***

> ***"I am not unidentifiable, not soulless."***

What burr scrounges to put me in raring yet defuses my rapier wit? Dear Zephyr denotes sapid Chianti of the lower Loire Valley. She's a lovely wassail that invigorates sparkling with floral notes, peach and pear, a Sunday *penuche* aperitif, a *ratafia*, that tetty cake with suavely foraging Sartori cheese or plum dessert.

***Talus…***

> ***"Let us see at once these incredulities, His forsaken kingdom."***

Men come to keep her playful prey, the sudden choking kinship bred of fear that supersedes all personal tastes. Mark their yelping cur noises. Now befalls a darker day. Soon her prey is cosset once claques inhale her rose tattoo and weigh not the spiny briar. Claudius can't see beyond the render; his awe is strewed with cheeky hoax and fiddly flowers. Still I feel the red but what chills are so frigid upon these wiles? Of covetous admire you feed too much on this delight. You arrive most puerile upon your bane. Life is never more callow than to wend one's way to be towed away. What spite foretells the coming day? To bear witness the betrayal and forbidden usury over north arc an ancient door obelus is bestead hung. In these incredulities is the palsied kingdom; the bribery of Judas submits in truth the disciple's pedant is undoing. We abhor the caitiff and all holier throng. Heaven is defiantly mute in earthy slumber as sophist fallaciously hinders fair course. The rather of it by these arguments set forth in your feckless pursuit, by my troth even the gist, banish your usury, I cannot praise thy riotous wisdom.

***Claudius…***

> ***"Are descended angels among us deposed to manful shards?"***

I would sigh the lack of a thing I sought. If my sighs fail not but so abate the lamented air, thus a thousand sighs to save. Heaven sent us fleshy habit rather than happiness. Contented with habit what sigh I cannot see myself 'til heaven clears. We hast not happiness I do confess that sighs tell all matter and feel no love in this. Thou hast not loved there's no tarrying here. I forsake angles' wraithlike prayer still lilt nous, to play cat's cradle. It rankles to occlude my pursuit of satiable fair play and I shan't surly gawk. In no doubt do what thou wilt shall be defray of the law. Am I so much? Do you think I am myself a better man than I am? What is he more than another and altogether more tractable?

***Hector…***

> ***"Zephyr would have you believe the Lamb lies down with the Lion."***

What though aches pitying me? Mustn't we fear the peril as, yet its stilted art besmirches still? What of bêtise that protests truth? It's our stolid ancestor's staid bid to put quite down a sally retort, a fencer's riposte to garish fine reason. What though endeavor keeps in flight a wonted pace from aery cliff pursue such habit in rote chorus. There's something in this more than nature by what better purpose could a withal be even therewith and direct with me. I have lost all my mirth. Hear of good intent; now shall I straightly go anon to my older. To veil full purpose whose mantle veiled every blot be not deceived. Liars' mulct sullies his chary to debase the threat and kindle surrender. Into queer shudders in nervy arms doth lay his squabble. Thou may well in him behold the lunatic 'tis nobler to suffer. In betimes, Claudius' rueful bluster doest cast himself out and swaggers a seething come what may.

***Talus…***

> ***"Zephyr isn't weakened by absence and dawdled time spent."***

Is it not so, whilst hold, she found Paris' hiatus afar clear of within? What casual fermata segues to next natter, nay caution? Beware ye, Hector, if once fallen, for ye shall lie in fascine long bundles, revetments for ditches in Scotland's fitting haugh. Though recusant she cannot raffish inter my torpor an unswerving life.

*Hector…*

> ***"Talus loiters alit at these dulcet words, jauntily spoken."***

It is indeed a caveat, fetching duende to surge my ghost with quelling vow. With raffia basket slung over her arm it's a mad rejoicing a grateful timeshare for life. She looks rich and privileged. Doesn't a harvest gypsy boast in spiel to illicit entrancing to spill out winds from these lineage sails? Randy thoughts delay leaving as confrere gathers wit to speak. Self-will resigns with the wit and judgment too. It may occur when trivial foray was all too subtle and tepid sparking-need a body cry-was most all agreeable. We're held slant by bounded days, of how laurels fade away, only yesterday was the sometimes in my dreams.

*Talus…*

> ***"Be not mute but come fay lithe." (Fay ce que vouldras, do what you like.)***

Nor never for my urging his pernicious life does what you like. Who shall be true to Claudius when we are so unsecret to ourselves? Say worst shall be a mock for his truth but what truth can speak truest? I'll rant as well as impeded this label to another maudlin deed. As poor player, no words ought to offend our hearing to hush some good pastime sweet with the fume of sighs. Remember how on past ineluctable beginnings that love contrived doest displease. To any lover and his cause to trawl, has he my thoughts, the gaff may be woeful to that end. Claudius owes merest to his ease, truly where it ought to be merely so, but with irascible aura how his anchored berth doest wreaths adder into his edacious mood.

***Claudius…***

> ***"What scorns man's immortal souls: whether whips of battle or whilst keen on frill and blind asunder to deserving shame?"***

To lay the blame my own despair, taunts and blame I laid upon myself or will you lay the fault on me? Does not become a man 'tis much the blame? My loins gentle and manners being of maid yet roused over with the virgin crimson of modesty, blame us not. For lesser knowledge, how accursed how unspoken enmities give way to rancor. Seaways blow currents inconstant and grades bend my mind. Blandish south winds hug pressing her diaphanous peignoir wrap in fawning form. White sails tumid full of ocean waft, indefensibly I stand luff under these feral winds. Mustn't we requite the emeute, the glory and the dream? Talus, dear brother, we are more alike than unalike. But not like our father, we are like these times we live in. Isn't it nobler to private wonders we seek?

***Hector…***

> ***"Claudius, we must indubitably depart in much due haste."***

Chimera is unsparingly *articulo mortis*. Wily smiles kindle to hoy me. Thou canst not smile forsooth this foppish schoolmaster. It's a biting skit what contempt whatnot to sway past my spike and brad. Razed out me welcome the stroke of death the bitter bread of banishment my comfort imparts will take our souls. Death is now my neighbor! Are we not affected suborn perjury to desultory ruse like wrath in death and envy afterwards? I'd scarcely trust myself as subtle masters do, I am enrapt a sad prophet where margent on salty shore I grieve at grievances tempter sent. It's a recital in ghoulish charade to come sadly as comely bliss is not apt at risk. Menander's locus: we live, not as we wish to, but as we can. Where life has no more interest, death should let life bear its name, inconsolable tears to that I call.

***Claudius…***

> ***"We cannot indubitably. Talus is burnishing white with fear."***

Yea, ilk the baleful louche of life's dismal title is, it shall come returning to rile common weal. To hold my foolish rival place for 'tis my rival father likes to wink at me. I'm so near the manners of my mother. If my desires be endless, my fears too will be so. What reason ever thusly salted my desires? I weep for joy my gentle calm, my ravenous senses. Mock not my conjuring under stinging nettles. Mockery wrenches are as keen as death. Chide your trespass and return your mock for it is as plain to say 'tis the spirit of hell. Mocking misery plays sports then shall he be mocked for his tresspass. You would laugh me. To make a loathsome abject scorn of me most untoward knave I shall spurn fate. I'm a zealous votary to fond desire but not to foolish tender. Is it not so, my instincts are strut set against the scouring gale? Then let wise abstaining befriends me, Hector dear brother, and I shall give you reason and fear in a handful of dust.

*Talus…*

> ***"What penance returns faith, to hand over title-soul to Him? Its God's own rogue, sackcloth and ashes. Alas, we shall die."***

From *ab inito*, our father's heritage, shorn of youth, feigns us requite. How fain I hated braved brother who worse hated mankind's meddlers. He taunts me you aptly will suppose what sharp wit he reasons to mitigate the scorn. What this diablerie did give us he bears himself proudly peruser of the ode. Whilst a thousand daggers added in my thoughts to upbraid in riot, I must withhold my riotous unrest. The days draw nigh wherein the dearth of freedom stay I have no pleasure in them. Thou the muzzle of restraint doth choke the unexpected courage of ignorance I'll trouble you no more. The patient soldier of fewer lots is docked to scanner; amplifiers *in situ* hymn a shortened canto. *Comme il faut*, as it should be, weakens any likelihood of fortune's chance, I did recoil. All that was there will be there still.

***Hector...***

> ***"It's imminent vile iniquity. Talus read God's ding scripture. For sake of exemption, icon alas, its God's first felony gag."***

Is undue *Ciao* slatternly burlesque? Is it not quite mocking indeed that we, slaves to frowsy sway, are patent chattel? In drab fret, we flagging bawds inveigled in her smarmy self doest waver. To dote was blamed as my curiosity than as pretence of unkindness. Isn't it aptly so that looming malice is a pang of conscience? How shall I lose the pang yet keep the sense for what thin partitions divide sense from what manner design where Julius and Pompey die. As whetted roué is honed invulnerable, dalliance gaily treads. But for dreaming on this naughty warder canst thy not winnow out what is seen true? To be wise in want and endure in weakness exceeds my might. Teach me to feel another's woe, to hide the fault

I see, that mercy shows to others that mercy gives to me. With my regrets, so also my contrary scruples are ending erroneous. Scoff my untoward blather.

***Talus…***

*"My avid pitching guard died aborning congress."*

**(Talus, too, succumbs and yields to Claudius' leeway)**

Fervent howls mote hard at my ref sentry and miffs the mind's eye. To no avail, I wait tiff and galling inane at costive thoughts rebuffed and blown flotsam. As friars once stood, as I bonhomie before her mystic lure, uprightness scorns my distrusting cur. My heart doth joy in my life I found no man, but he was truer to me. A prize no less in worth, we must keep him safe and give him all kindness. How everything is changed. Aren't literal minds grateful indeed that legerdemain cannot garrote love's gift of oneself? Life's thirst in full blush waits not to see plain desires when love congeals. Thou seek now a wharf burly on the quay to moor imparts fondling so near. Sated life abides swains ever yearn to unfailing stardust.

***Hector…***

> ***"Ne plus ultra is beggared."***

**(Be both in person of duties and compassion)**

As caution's heed subsides, their bounds divide, wayfarer wits are sure to folly. If you are solitary, fully idle be not blithely to sluggard's comfort. Whenever our minds are pressed close against duties and sorrows, instinct enlightens the unfolding course and gentle truce and the usual play. But when contention and occasion meet *Ne plus ultra* pay heed is a bequeathal flame; alluring flame that burns to endow us for a lifetime, else unattended ashes for thirty. Claudius and no-one else must say sanely tomorrow and prophetically be conceited that he raves in saying still his resilient vim. He is so plague proud. My mind is troubled by these cudgeling sinews and I myself see not the bottom of it. Man is led astray by faintest reason, save for, it is wise to deem the heart. This undying ukase indeed addles my mind. Come to fate that gave you breath, *nosce te ipsum.*

***Claudius…***

> ***"Prepare my death throes; anoint me in rich meridian oil."***

**(Claudius announces life choice, not defeat)**

Perpend my boding ways of uninspiring term as touched she brushed my hand, just once. I see intense wild roses, purple-rimmed blooms, and funeral lisianthus. I define humanity, as such: we cannot find peace by avoiding life. Horace taught "*Non-sum qualis eram*", we are not as then. He wrote "*Omnia vincit amor*", love conquers all. Most inalienable and dear in use, now shall we see tomorrow. What mended values likely to succeed are we looking for? We construe to have control over prospects and means to pursue it. But when are dreams attainable and when nonplus 'tis suffused farcical? Unmastered importunity and impatient mind but that's the measure, isn't it? Throughout all retorting rule my scuffed morals welter undo hours, and hereafter I shan't be thistle uncouth whilst things left hindmost undone. Take the pathway for extol travels in a straight so narrow. Is it not a wonder well-nigh a strange fellow? Life must be patterns of episodes, lingering memories, faiences to add laughter and opaque luster. If tomorrow be a fair day, if fountains of your mind were clear again, then welcome laud and charity as tempera all to my twilight saga. Whatever dreams may come to puzzle my will 'tis far better than he himself might quietuses make. Whichever I can flaunt for fardel-life hence to come, I opine, we shall find treatise of this night, unfurl its ever glow. Where it burns, the bell then beating one, comport and bring her beauty to the stars' tumult by the same covenant that usurps this night.

***Hector…***

> ***"Claudius, we shall find comfort for your adorable Mother."***

Mistrust of my success hath done this deed. Now I see thou art a fool and fit for thy master, I am your fear for that. Coyness turns intemperate ennui; these calumnies subject all is not soon conceived. Let that appear till now so much it's he himself what tells this fawning for lout's budding ill repute. I'll come no more behind your scene to excite the wicked penchant, a time so naked to wispy rumpus rather than wary thought. The kneading, the making of cake, the patron's ruth to let pass all for virtue who never handled a rod would soon displace my fleeting liberty. Tell the salt marshes and beat on your drum; tell me what English virtue brings us together else what gotten beatitudes tear us apart. I can't contrive ere a mayhap but mark this parvenu as woman and aver partaking there's neither fleeing nor flight from this indubitable hunger. Fie this pining! For who firmly decided regards us however else resolved there shall we for joy gain or sadly forfeit. But summon proud fate the left hand of lot and let fiat being done to cut away the cancer of bent. Whenever we are as base as come what may, Aristotle, whenever we seek an anonymous perhaps, the farce is played out. So are you churl to my thoughts. Alas 'tis a pity without my sluice to jetty come roiling sea, she befalls by night a knowing look, ripening breath upon her poise, consigns a poor player his sweet afters. To speak the rites of marriage, what tale this mingled yarn, I have wail fully despaired.

With mirth and with dirge in marriage farewell and let your haste acclaim your duty. Sift curtly throughout what is useful. Thus, much the business is we have here writ. Listen carefully, dear Claudius, we cannot step into these same waters twice; it is certain in time gentle occasions ebb and flow onward to others. Take hold of virtue, the cause and precious time within our imminent reach. The same gravitas good to the very outrance I can consent. Alas, we must discern if shipwright bewails salient gist, he's never quite with cut and bowsprit jib. The arc of human compassion is quite long, I accuse, and it bends to love. Virtues are lost for want of asking. Beauty, truth and rarity love hath reason but thereon reason none else. What doth her beauty serves, doff thy name. It's nature's double name; it is a wonder as chorus to their tragic scene keep the obsequy so strict lest the requiem lacks right. If to woman, he be bent as liege man use his company no more. I'd not believe them more. Take her hence in horror would go all disquieted countenance. Reason in itself confounded in truth but in love's fasting pain cannot be; as fickle fortune smile 'tis her infirmity and beauty bury be to this urn.

***Claudius…***

> ***"Goodbye Hector, farewell Talus dear friend. Ides of March. I cannot escape. Pithy liberty woe adieu…"***

**(It is as it should be)**

Silly wanly, boys, I gave cede gladly and had twice wrongly despaired. *Comme il faut*, as it should be. This day I breathed first, time is come around. As 'tis now where I begin, there shall I end. But this day must end what works the Ides of March began our everlasting farewell takes. My inward soul the night forestalls me the coming day. I can dream all alone in the moonlight. Dreaming moonlight will hide my joy no longer. Sorry dreaming but nature wants gleaming in keen youth to drive away dark dismal dreaming nights. I canst not look warily that dies in tempest 'tis good morn smiles on a frowning night. I must wait for the sunrise soon it will be morning. Another day is dawning, and the wind begins to moan another day will begin. You'll understand what happiness is, a new day has begun. There's no way to deny it love shines once more like it did before. No regrets. To be revenged upon her with trencher, old tedious fools abaft the beam, prating the more pity laid on my duty. We shall smile, why then, this parting was well made. Dread nothing. Before love's dreams new yearn and I defend for whom, then, shall I henceforth live if not for her? Unfold yourself speak to it as though art to thyself 'tis odd. Let it be tenable and whatsoever else give it an understanding as mine to you. Fie! 'Tis a fault as to reason most absurd. The dram in nature cannot choose its origin as infinite as man may undergo. Be they as pure as grace their virtues or else fortune's star in their birth as to manner born to cast thee up again, we're fools of nature. Thus, said and no more.

**END**

# CESAREAN'S BAD MISTRESS

BY THOMAS LEPERA

Oh, what a deal of scorn looks stun in the contempt and anger on my lips. Is fault not itself shown more soon than whence love seems most hidden? I myself, Cesarean, by the sweetest roses of early spring, by maiden's honor, truth and everything else humanly dear I love thee so it muggers all my pride nor wit nor reason can my passion hide. Do not extort thy reasons for that I woo, thou therefore hast no cause, but woo with reason fettered. Love sought is good but given unsought better. There is something good in everything I see. In the firelight every minute is an eternity. I have a dream a fantasy to help me through reality. The time is unreal for me. Tell me what's wrong. Mulling it over is there no hope for tomorrow?

Nothing lasts forever except the memory of betrayal. There're rosemary sprigs for remembrance rue my heart. Worse and worse mistress made malleable born to undo us. The ache of denial from my unfilled grasp as once held a perfect face but wife has thoughts of fey wanderings gone cursed. Winter's kisses pairs of cast lips, rare courtier, sabotage to no avail. These rashes urge thou set amid us how flair taken is but wafted *flagrante delicto* too hastily cut out for her. Willful consenters' do distraught me. My wife comes foremost a tribute then molts a lunatic. Lunatics bestrew them. Such haughty burlesque stands up and swings right back. It is a facial frown of rebuff how I tell of lustful play to every duty. Her brow summit, temples scowl grimace, then speak in shrill tones the cuff of denial is overruled by the clout of each dire betrayal.

Why then 'tis time now to smile again. Oh, how inaptly the poor player be not contrived. Should sorrow be ever razed yet testy wrath conceited with sweet fumes of white lilacs to upbraid me so to sneer lower a crazed mind. A smoldering firedamp is apt to loathe staidly one so dour and I forlorn how toll our cheeky lady. A maid suborned for wife a roiling sea bestirred in strange maladies to rouse the rutty play. My wife shall meet with better dreams. For wooing here is offered love my fishwife to take in her mistress. She brings her figs and when to the lute, she sung and made the night bird mute that still records with moans; nobly let us prepare some welcome for the mistress of the house. Fair angel hasn't wooed me I rail what days' éclat whilst I am a beggar. I shouldn't deny so many talents had she mistaken her and sent to me, a fever longing still to commend me to thee, laid bases to make us heirs to all eternity.

The mistress a servile maid yet I'm arrest whining still to stand wake at intermissions. Be not afraid, good youth, I shan't have you. And when youth is come to harvest, we're alike to reap a proper way. To compass wonders the near course laid out is not mine to have. There lies your way, due west. The devil cannot plague her better adventurous by desire whom none resist. To discourse thee unlikely wonders enacted more than a man as I am now but by help of devils do contend testy rivals so astray and more suitors to taste inflamed desire.

Give mistress one gentle kiss the more for joy of this sad news. I'll claim that pledge at mistress' hands to yield under all unlade gameness. As the devil's fiddle tempts virtue, wilt not thou do torment me thus?

Whence did see mistress' zeal will prove the appetite of my eye to ogle an engaging repast to swear a most splendid feast. Come let us sup' in betimes that afterward here we may digest our complots in some variety. Let the locksmiths do his craft to fashion a wellbeing belt: discretion of pure chastity must be fitted foremost where my empathy begins and ends with my wife who cannot break away from herself famished to fondle in dike relief her mistress. Hand her the key. I'll be the lonely cheater by reason which fact I infer, and they shall be East and West very virtuous sisterhood whence comes I trade to them both.

On my wife's frailty, I cannot doff aside morality but now to know its qualm. Wife too unkind be that hereafter to leave ugly scars where all lies fester. Is it that I have looked upon deceit grown to such excess? Rue the tears I shed to do worse to felled rabble. Well, I conceive do not give dalliance too much the rein. But how should I deserve as ill as you and make me a fellow tribune? Worthy tribune is chosen; take a chance on me. Striving tribune can't thou tell to brave a hearing give way send thee by me. The winner takes it all. Aye evermore contempt frail dwelling house forsooth I am a coy rascal, a puny knave in profiting by them my desires for sport as men have. Never dismay these fables or these fairy toys. If one be, so are they all; all union flatterers yearn to dip in the same bawdy dish. Two lovers' colliery has I to them strive to let worthless stuff excite our awe in my infamy inured to despair.

How bent wretched boughs defile my laurels. Spare not this Quean, I forbid her my house. Consort damned for beguiling the devil but he shall have his bargain. I dare abide timidity no longer. In my manor, plushy among us with riches I grapple to choose which feint to pay employ, but omens possess it and so mock this day. What cast aspersion shall the heavens let fall to deny the bond. For thou shall find she will outstrip the weight of governance and make primacy halt behind her, alas my trials of love hast strangely stood apart. What madness may come festering wretched fools let crass rawness live on to coarse wants. In plangent bays they fester with puling airs. I had from these confines called to enact my quaintly passion tenured in moans.

Never till this day quieted after everyone had gone to indulge in moiré ripple irregular waves to know we are such stuff as dreams are made on. What grating rogues and doting sightseers are we overwhelmed by iniquity now must bid a fare thee well my liege thou art a gallant youth. No more care-free laughter, this is where the past ends. This time we are sorely through nothing more to say amidst sorrow knowing you is the best I can do. All my sins lack mercy. But quid for quo and free all faults there is no mercy will breathe within your lips. You must not dare whose dimpled smiles from fools which steals itself there is no mercy left. Come torn asunder my untried lure as dying cinders lie heaving, I am quite the piffling caretaker, alas a distempered guest. Devil himself spoke of what shameful odyssey to see hunger daring to tour in raw jollies. Shame and delusion are in the rout of men. It trebles my chilling injury to think of otherwise of those eyes awry a mistress and yourself.

Worse than my name what hast this fortune on me but brought to nothing. To crave your mercy wilt thou my consort consent. Thou pardon me my wrongs for my mad mistaking I pardon crave of thee sweet lady. Whom for this time we release we enjoin thee and hope I had grace. Another place another time may you fall from this wreckage and find comfort here. Speak so gently I condemn not from nature stolen my improper abuse reprehending thee. Commend me to thy care I cannot get. Let's exchange its charity go thy old woman into the chamber let pandering adduct me then in me abide. Do as I bid take me on. That she this day shame cast take on me all mischance scoffs grew shameless in despite were not enough. A thing loves in my despite what mortality might rail endeavor anything. What mine own deposed nature shall be notwithstanding above all else who can withstand you? Ay, why not? Unmake is that misfortune hath followed me. In what jeering contempt of man did lend, I frown on my bitter penury.

**END**

# WITCHES OF ENDAU

BY THOMAS LEPERA

Once a fortnight there comes a brindle fog creeping afar then to near. A brindle vapor soaked in fright licked its tongue into the corners of this dreadful night. A fortnight ill but what inkling have I this fortnight been? None but witches those fags on winged flight do settle herein. By the mere prodding of her cleft finger amazing evil this may come. Midnight hags what is it you must do? Rising up spirits though dead from ground demanding that lodging be unsettled what a dire fry throughout this dismal trial is at Christian door. What mischief work sees here thou dead had tint of earthly flesh? Wert once stained stalwart earthy life-beams standing unsure whose rightful cause reigns no more.

I may tell pale-hearted fear that lies and sleeps in spite of thunder.besides the gory banquet three witches that are to come has my fear aright. For tasty ingredients of their cauldron add a succulent finger and tongue full of flavor and perhaps a yummy ear and liver of cursed Turk. Pesto of Farer's lips makes the gruel thick then the allure is firm and able. Now the cauldron sings enchanting all that she had put to time unending convention be avid with ardent touch what cauldron fruits what magic charm is this? Into the cauldron boil and bake ears of cat, tongue of goat, lizard's eyeball and owlet's wing. It makes of such gripping potion raise like consommé simmer poison and bubble hell-trouble. Drinking off this potion is a sleeping elixir, loathed medicine.

Come to Endau they will surely do us no harm but for this heap of barmy flesh. Soul killing witches shall deform the corps with roots of dark hemlock silvered by the moon's eclipse. Hags have gossamer wings such 31ft span in vein of archangels mighty warlike vista. Chough of red legs and glossy blue-black plumage, fulsome green catlike eyes with sharp golden-spiked talons onset poor Harvey Mayfield's site, menacing to see, they'll soon have his false-teeth in a jar to sport on rare occasions. Hags are undaunted to wearing loose-fitting plates. Sisters smirk to taut delights how mercy o'me that a host of witches' thunderous hilarity does fill this Christ memorial park. Under the gods keep your awe which else would feed on one another? What stinking breaths. Nay then such wanton lies, veiled in dames' spoils, get my resolve.

Thoughts to content do flatter themselves in refuge their shame bearing their own trial before endured the like. What though afflicts the object of misery we scruple men cannot content but for revenge thirst as on we seek reprisal to the end. Do you hear, master porter, I shan't ready you now. Keep the gate open 'til then heard call from me. On my Christian conscience, this banquet that is to come will beget a thousand more, damned bloody works of despicable fondle. Weird sisters, Artois, Walloon and Picardy this mournful night is secured having all day to carouse fitting deceit conceived in baleful sorcery; this heinously foul spectacle alas to come. Doest you hear, master porter, I have two pence to transmit me across.

Whence find the other side please accept payment due and row me there. To arm! To arm! The sister doth make assault. Make haste if it chances the one of us do fail the other may rise against their force. What surfeits relieve us if they would not yield? Let us revenge this with spikes. Sergeants draw your sword for we shan't join with witches and the aid of hell. Be bloody, bold and resolve; chortle to scorn for none of woman born shall harm. Be lion-mettle, proud and take no care; we shall never bested be. Cry 'courage' to all the currents of a heady fight and challenge their depraved sovereigns.

Our business is not unknown they have had inkling this fortnight what we intend to do. My good friends' honest neighbors will you undo yourselves? I tell you friends you're suffering in dearth but well strike with your staves curse them as enemies. They are not such as you. These unseasoned hours perforce must add unto your valiant courage and undaunted spirit. Strut with courage enough do not fear the flaw. Upon the footing of our land worthy courage may meet a prouder foe. Grapple with her ere she comes so nigh. As ever was laid the time itself unsorted we are not petty cowardly knaves. We lay aside our faults and ruth I beseech you they shan't pass. Mad about our throwing very ancient persevere intact to withstand danger proves my title. Our virtue is to make us worthy whose offences subdue and not curse that justice did it. Lay down the command dauntless spirit of decided rule. In truthful sooth they are our dire demur. Tell the clock we benefit the hour shall be my precedent to draw the sword. A biting sword in work is rah to mark their gauzy wings. Though time foresees the danger we send forth be rough and razorable whose every cubit seems to cry out do discharge upright fortune. And look how well my garments set upon me. Direst cunning does tempt me further draw thy sword give them instant tidings. Though fires burn and cauldron bubble I conjure you by that you profess vile witches fear the sword. Forfeit by the law 'tis too late should she stoop in pity. On some great sudden hest what portents are these? Become not one half in graces as pity does should she kneel in mercy. The watchful hour cheered up the heavy time we must not dare for shame to talk of mercy. I am no mourner for that news they have been still mine enemies. And I shall laugh to tell thee to look upon their tragedy. Therefore, rouse up fear and trembling and do rite to my spite. This way you have well expounded it and give today a tiara. Scale of tooth of witches' gulf she that would be wanton slayer now scuttles from you as night breezes what first fill gossamer wings do wither pall this cursed night with dreadful fright. So went on the strength of our amity. How foolish doth a fear seems now? I warrant safe in sooth and sound upon my sword with raucous resounding trumps' bray make us step first to shout and cry out "Hallelujah!". To our glory singing Hallelujah!!

**END**

# WILY RABBIT

BY THOMAS LEPERA

Royal hydrangeas, radiant thistle, white blazing star where meadows are refulgent in wild flowers make our private wilds home. West Virginia highlands can be a wonderful and star tingly mystery, a landscape to explore serene wilderness, untamed life utterly untroubled in full autumnal glory. It was one perfect autumn day which occurs more frequently in memory than in life. In late October, fall colors add to pictorial golf course at the Backwoods Resort. Kujo the Cat and Mr. Eric are busybodies together chase windblown sere yellow leaves and yap a childlike bliss at the rabbit playing golf on the 15$^{th}$ green.

He's a most curious sight lithe visage sporting an Englishman's bowler hat and smoking a Churchill strut cigar. He wears pleated lapful kilt, leather linked belt and Gaelic long knee socks of Scottish green heritage embroidered in gold RSA crest and yellow top-tassels. Curled wisps of circum smoke loop and hoop about in the air. A murder of crows touts aloud whilst perched near above on limb of an elm utter their gaiety. It isn't awry spoof that the rabbit is putting a golf ball rather Kujo's quixotic sarcasm is that the golf clubs surely must be rented.

Eric loves his surrogate son and says nothing at the risible idea. Mr. Rabbit, too, takes small notice of man and cat as he skillfully dropped a thirty-footer. Some foist perhaps, perhaps a miracle comes? Father and son herald this éclat virtuoso moreover clever but fata morgana vision came to nonplus. Rabbit abruptly turning with lark shunts unsparingly aimed at fat Kujo the Cat.

Solipsist Rabbit chortling *"O' days too sweet too bright tae last are yea indeed forever past? Across the moonlit heather roaming I go musardy in Almost Heaven. In fields of homing caddie, the joy I yare know at leisure will confess nosh measure."*

What can we make of this animus display? Was wily Rabbit's singing his chaste anthem his own paean? Well, operas should only be played for foreigners, they wrote it. Orneriest rabbit suum cuique aplomb with every putting stroke profuse with orgulous pride couldn't utter a single howdy do. Ugly rabbit undeniably biased by incidental luck. Is churlish bad the new cool? He didn't even tip his English bowler hat, a nettled discourtesy twice smarmy unfamiliar in these parts but common in Italy. What foreign accent was that? "Hey there, what's your name, Rabbit?" With unceasing wriggles and visceral twists, gave no answer.

But wily Rabbit hastily exclaimed, *"It's my valiant putter that cannot miss full the maun mark in a hundred, thousand auditions." "Perfect deeds are born bonhomie taken as a whole made restive by fu' tassie and maut dram." "Nay foozles it, aye."*

Well, this kind of shoddily manner wasn't to be taken lightly… no sir. Mr. Eric said, "Rabbit, I can cause you to miss, *tae* wince." Sly Rabbit stodgily drubbed, *"And quite so, and should a fly bit a thoroughbred it would surely wince. But the fly is an insect all the same a pest; the thoroughbred a stately horse, still."*

As father and son quibbled, they decided to render their own naked derrieres, a repaying logy gesture. "What bloody good sport, Dad." "Tit for tat, as 'twere". What now there you have it nowhere else whilst the fête scene is put fat Kujo the Cat, Mr. Eric and wily Rabbit mooning unabashedly one another. A murder of crows' barks in shirks, baying guffaws, at the unfolding macaws' drama to shilly-shallying around.

I do not secure myself in a foolish thought to say a sorry sight. But yea, subject to your countenance glad or sorry where you were tied in duty. How I may bestow myself to be regarded in duty. A woman sometimes scorns what best contents her but not for duty of the game. Bestow not these fawning smiles but I think my patience and my wrath shall far exceed what coy smiles ever irk my game. A woman golfer is a notable milestone of an embalmer's art.

Every so often as mercurial occasion would insist writ of it attending hammy drama takes on a new inexplicable reality. Was this sully manner of pointing slapdash or slipshod to be a novel way of saluting? Unruly sun, now the moon walks the bright night in her silver *arse shoon*. Rabbit is probably from Troon or Carnoustie, everyone in Edinburgh is brain-damaged. Was this signal a prurient divine rite of passage? Yet rights of announcing mores is not MacDuff original stuff. To coin a phrase, wily Rabbit choose fittingly the immutable Scottish "Show-thus-far" to name his masterful putting whilst we thought wrongly to name his rear end gyrating aimed unabashedly.

Wily Rabbit said, *"Das we think making bonnie fools of ourselves is less real and true than tae behave sensibly? They are incontestably real; they are the only things schawys that are due humanly true. What do we ever get from of wotted reading tae equal the excitement and revelation in thegither first fourteen years? After this age, belated books hurl meaning through time and dark space reveals them a Trojan horse. Memory is embalmed oftentimes bloody censured beyond recognition, lamented only when anyone still notices it's gone. The time tae taste adulthood is never; psychoses are pitiable with murky cases. 'Tis aye swathe no doubt ta retain ya waiflike humor and gleaning boyish wit."*

The truth of this collaborator Rabbit wanted the best of innocence. Innocence is novel, full of glee and unstained. Trite is boring, clichéd and stayed. Commerce is surly trite. Spalding ruined all with ladies golf bags. Spalding's bags have tiny pockets slotted for a towel, soap, mirror, teasing hair spike for pleated corn rows, pink golf tees and balm lipstick. Women golfers are two-thirds mush and one-third Eleanor. She is unfitted for golf. Her norms are elastic and rash with the scoring. She has no special awareness and is malignant, scheming sort of quipster. Since a woman never believes what she is saying, she is quite surprised when other believe her. Just say the word woman golfer and I think of chicanery. Nobody discerns otherwise either to genuflect or spit. The ultimate worth of any woman golfer is to raise man's suffering to an elevated bleak level.

Rabbit said, *"Can you imagine such claptrap asinine twaddle? Its jowl howler sold anywhere else. Rest assured there's no such getting, not a wee wail, of this gobbledygook in Scotland's highlands. In golf the game submits tribute name in its innocence. Whatever happened to yesteryear when club members were closely partial by invitation only?" Take the sweet of my innocence. I doubt not then but innocence shall make spotless the commerce of fools."*

What wants are these that bear these scorns? State a moral case to a ploughman to decide it well for he has not been led astray by mock caucus. We fret Mahoun's law and test Murray's divine worries. But to expose charity of miracles affable human spirit springs forth from raw life. By and large I'm sadly outvoted by din madness as its caucus adheres to civil liking. Do we not always follow customs of ecumenical contumely if once you don't want to give or receive scandal? Church edicts and Picasso's art confuse me: sainthood is mainly the redound telling of insane people; and Andy Warhol's watery art was a tomato can. The whole delirium of man's quest of religion and Picassoesque art consists aye in discussing if it exists. Animated mimicry is yentle dovecotes of mental disturbances. Comfy isn't it? We must be more thoughtful of exacting useful purpose. It's more explicit pratfall but not widely accredited.

The forename "show-thus-far" is a far better substitute than the taunting lexis "scooting the greens fantastic" once aired on ABC's World of Sports. In fairness to feral life Kujo the Cat is the unique self to have ever authored to have ever mimicked his Father in such surprising detail. Since then eccentric faux pas have given twists to original text, but now alien version. The disingenuous camarilla today had adopted the shortened dialect as *Shofar*, the goat horn trumpet blown to announce the garrison Rite of Passage or upbraid some minatory thing, some craven paradigm or rout restraint. We are free to theorize with all abandon that comes of immunity to the facts. Stand in the thrill of all immunity slammed by all the scrutiny but too late for fate it comes.

The Backwoods Resort retains an air of awe in contrast. These hills, the out-and-out shape and heft of them with long views and temperate beauty, have bucolic lushness in valley floors with wandering brooks. Its pieces of alluring landscape gripping beyond language speak with a bell voice. Muttering with liberal infer every grateful player is besotted in dazed sentiment by a neighborhood of profuse fairways and spectacular scenery. And elsewhere there's a nearest and dearest store down the road a bit where you buy cinnamon-apple pies and prize cherry pies and chocolate cream pies. And all too welcome tete a' tete brings a warm sundry. Now we have at long last the whole unheralded adjuvant story, we think. Even though ambiguity guards access to West Virginia mores in most folderol testimonial, today we view *Shofar*- a commove reenactment- as golfers gather round to moon unabashedly one another with animated keenness shunting side to side on the 15th green, Backwoods Resort, West Virginia.

This shining biography now widespread as fibbing and hardly less culpable has a crimson thread of kinship running through us all. In these mores before calumny's worst clobber can we depart from our pitifully ethnicity for sake of the splendid good? Some weird guy demurring his emollient best with morbid humor, perchance someone less rooted less aptly suited, conceivably a strayed waddie walker said that every year inexorably on September 21st, near or about, impudent wily Rabbit's striking image is quite discernibly joyful. Playing golf wearing his Englishman's bowler hat and smoking his Churchill strut cigar, he sings a homily song:

> ***"Mister blue bird's on my shoulder. It's the truth, it's actual, everything's satisfactual. My oh my what a wonderful day. Plenty of sunshine coming my way. Zippity doo dah, zippity aye."***

As prisoner bird's thralldom must find in freedom and I was filled with such delight, he breathed this song into the air, for who has sight so keen and strong that it can follow the flight of song. Song is the breathing rose bold with sweets in every sheathing fold. I should be sorry to have that voice fall silent alas and *aye* pass out of my life.

Yes, wily Rabbit really did and continues hither and thither to make that thirty-footer without tort fall short. ***"Wait for me yare way I shall return ae day".***

**END**

www.ingramcontent.com/pod-product-compliance
Lightning Source LLC
Chambersburg PA
CBHW020121130526
44591CB00031B/251
* 9 7 8 1 9 4 9 3 6 2 6 8 8 *